Historical Etchings
FARMING

Copyright-free illustrations for lovers of history

Compiled by
Bobbie Kalman

 Crabtree Publishing Company

Historical Etchings Series

In 19th-century North America, hundreds of artists produced black-and-white steel-plate and woodcut engravings for newspapers, periodicals, books, and catalogs. Over a period of more than five years, Bobbie Kalman and Peter Crabtree traveled to libraries throughout North America to research these etchings for Crabtree Publishing Company's *Early Settler Life* series. Researching etchings meant working in climate-controlled rooms to make sure the pages of the old newspapers and books in which these etchings appeared did not crumble due to age and dryness. Special photographers had to be hired and approved.

Many of the etchings in the *Early Settler Life* series have never appeared in other collections, so Bobbie is often asked for permission to use them. By popular demand, they have been gathered into a series of their own: the *Historical Etchings* series. Today, although many of the original sources and creators' names are forgotten, these illustrations offer a fascinating glimpse into the daily lives of the settlers of North America.

Crabtree Publishing Company

350 Fifth Avenue	360 York Road, RR 4	73 Lime Walk
Suite 3308	Niagara-on-the-Lake	Headington
New York	Ontario, Canada	Oxford OX3 7AD
N.Y. 10118	L0S 1J0	United Kingdom

Cataloging in Publication Data

Kalman, Bobbie
  Farming: copyright-free illustrations for lovers of history

(Historical etchings)

ISBN 0-86505-915-2 (pbk.)
This book contains etchings and accompanying text depicting various aspects of farm life in pioneer times, including chores, livestock, and harvests.

1. Agriculture—North America—History—Juvenile literature.
2. Farm life—North America—History—Juvenile literature.
3. Frontier and pioneer life—North America—Juvenile literature.
[1. Farm life—History. 2. Frontier and pioneer life.] I. Title.
II. Series: Kalman, Bobbie. Historical etchings.

S441.F25 1997   j630'.973   LC 97-31452

CIP

Contents

Many early settlers arrived in the New World with the dream of owning a farm. Before they could begin working the land, however, they spent months clearing the trees and huge boulders from it. Strong animals such as oxen helped with this tiring, difficult work.

The farmer is guiding a harrow, a wooden tool used to prepare fields for planting. Harrows had wooden or metal teeth that raked the earth and broke up the soil. On newly cleared land, harrows were easier to use than plows, which often got caught on stumps or old roots.

Earlier in the day this farmer set one of his fields on fire because ashes make good fertilizer. Unfortunately, the wind changed direction. Now the fire is out of control and spreading toward the house. The farmer and his family are fighting to keep back the flames.

Well-kept fences were especially important on pioneer farms. If a fence was damaged, an animal could escape and wander miles away from the farm. A valuable source of meat for the family could easily become dinner for a wild animal.

Not only was it difficult to keep animals in, it was also hard to keep people out of one's field. This farmer is posting a "No Trespassing" sign to ensure that people do not trample his wheat.

Most farmers kept pigs because they were inexpensive to feed. Pigs ate scraps from the family's meals. In some communities, pigs were let loose every morning to eat the garbage in the streets!

Geese often guarded a farm, especially when the farmer did not have a dog. These fierce birds honked loudly and nipped intruders with their strong beaks. This piglet is getting a real "goosing!"

Pigs ate everything in sight if they were allowed to roam. This farmer's dog was sleeping while the neighbor's pigs snuck into the pumpkin patch. Now the farmer's family won't have pumpkin pie for Thanksgiving!

A farmer and his family admire the flock. They are trying to decide which turkey they want to save for their Thanksgiving dinner. The rest will be taken to market and sold or traded for other goods.

Fashionable farmers fancied fluffy feathered fowl. Some raised several types of chickens as well as ducks, geese, and pigeons. The farmer who owns these fowl also raises rabbits.

This woman is feeding her flock. Most farms had at least one type of poultry. The birds were kept as a source of meat, eggs, and feathers. Their feathers were used to stuff mattresses, quilts, and pillows.

Sheep were a source of meat and wool. Each spring, the sheep's fleece was washed then sheared. Women combed the fleece and then spun it into yarn on a spinning wheel.

Cattle provided meat and milk for a farmer's family. Some of the milk was drunk. The rest was made into butter and cheese. Oxen were used to plow fields and pull heavy loads.

Some pioneer farmers could not afford to buy a dairy cow. They kept goats to provide milk and cheese for their family. Goats are like pigs—they eat just about any kind of food.

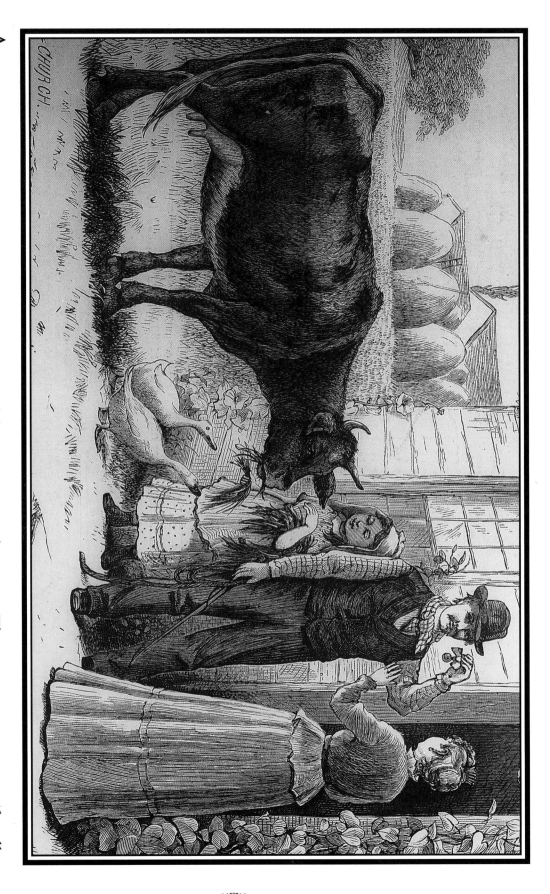

A farmer returns from the country fair with a medal. His cow won first prize. There were competitions for all types of livestock, as well as crops, baking, and farming skills such as plowing. Fairs gave farmers from different areas a chance to meet, discuss new farming methods, and see the finest livestock.

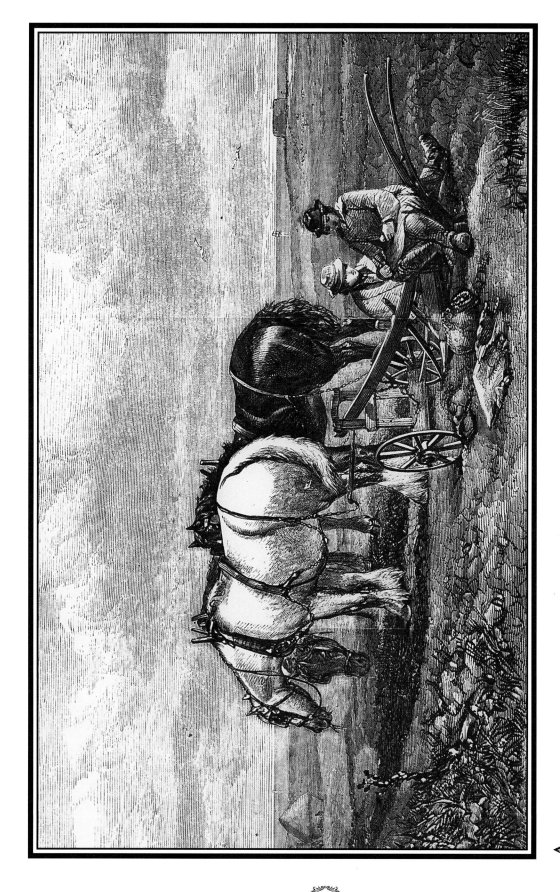

A team of workhorses or oxen was invaluable on early farms. These strong animals performed many important tasks, such as pulling harrows, plows, wagons, and sleds. They were able to pull heavy loads.

A young or wild horse had to be broken, or tamed, before it could be taught
to carry a rider or pull a load. It took many men to hold back a strong horse.
A fine-looking horse such as this one was often used to pull a carriage or cutter.

Cattle ranchers herded their cattle to new grazing lands or to market in large cattle drives. It was important to keep the herd from splitting up and strays from falling behind. Cattle were too valuable to lose!

Autumn was the time to harvest ripe pumpkins from the pumpkin patch. This family is choosing pumpkins for their jack-o'-lanterns. The brother and sister in front have a scary face in mind for their pumpkin. Mother is thinking about the pumpkin pie she will bake.

Families harvested their grain crops in late summer. Everyone helped with the grain harvests. The crop had to be gathered and moved indoors quickly, in case of rain. After the stalks were cut, they were raked, piled high on the back of a wagon, and moved to the barn for storage.

These families are working together at a haying bee. Everyone is relaxing after a delicious picnic lunch, which was prepared by the women. After clearing today's field, everyone will work hard to clear another neighbor's tomorrow.

After grain crops were harvested, the grains had to be threshed, or separated from the stalks. These farmers are working together to thresh their crops quickly. The horses on the left are being used to power a threshing machine. Beyond them, men are busy filling sacks with grain at another type of thresher.

This orchard belongs to one of the farmers who is picking peaches. His neighbors have come from miles away to help him harvest the crop. Later, they will enjoy a huge meal and dance to celebrate the end of their work.

This farmer has hired a couple of men from the village to help with his apple harvest. In exchange for their work, he will give them a meal and a share of the apples. His grandchildren are picking apples for their grandmother, who is in the house baking pies.

These children are carrying bushels of apples to the cider press. Their family will make apple juice, cider, and vinegar. They have already stored enough apples in the cellar for the family to use during the winter.

These illustrations show the steps involved in making cider. First, the apples are gathered. They are taken to a cider press, where the juice is squeezed from them. The juice is stored in large kegs and left to ferment.

A SUGAR BUSH AND CAMP.

SYRUPING DOWN.

EMPTYING THE BUCKETS.

Every year, a group of men returns to the sugar bush camp when it is time to begin maple sugaring. They tap the trees, collect the sap, and boil it to make syrup. The syrup is transported in huge barrels.

These men are busy boiling down sugar cane to make sugar and molasses. A few are chopping sugar cane in the fields while the rest work on the refining process. Sugar cane is still the major source of the world's sugar and molasses.

Wealthy young people from the cities flocked to the country to experience farm life. Farmers rented rooms and made money playing host to them. The guests preferred to relax, however, rather than do the work that was part of life on the farm.